MANAGING BACK-TO-SCHOOL ANXIETY

A Parent's Guide to Helping Our Children Worry Less

JESS HASTINGS-LESPERANCE

DEDICATION

With all my heart I dedicate this book to
my three children, Kolby, Arkelle, and Nash.

Each of you are inspiring and
strong, and I love being your mom.

Managing Back-to-School Anxiety
A Parent's Guide to Helping Our Children Worry Less
Second Edition

ISBN PRINT: 978-1-990352-84-3
ISBN EBOOK: 978-1-990352-85-0

Art Direction including Book Cover, Typesetting and Layout Design Copyright © 2023, LeadHer Publishing
Graphic Design - Christina Williams
Editing - Kim Collins

To find out more about Jessica Hastings-Lesperance, visit cedarwellnessstudio.ca

To find out more about the publisher, visit leadherpublishing.com

Disclaimer

The information in both electronic and paperback versions of this book, or on the linked websites included as reference material, is presented for educational purposes only. It is not intended as a substitute for the diagnosis, treatment, or advice of a qualified, licensed medical professional. The information presented are offered as information only, not medical advice, and in no way should anyone infer that we are practicing medicine. Seek the advice of a medical professional for proper application of this material to any specific situation.

The book does not contain health advice. The health information is provided for general informational and educational purposes only and is not a substitute for professional health advice. Accordingly, before taking any actions based upon such information, we encourage you to consult with the appropriate medical and healthcare professionals. We do not provide any kind of health advice. The use or reliance of any information contained in both digital and paperback versions of this book is solely at your own risk.

CONTENTS

FOREWORD

I first met Jessica in October of 2019 when my sister persuaded me to partake in a spin class with *"the amazing instructor"* she is so fond of. I was instantly hooked on the energy Jessica exuded in her spin and trauma-informed yoga class. I knew immediately that she would add a new dimension to my life. A couple of months after that, I began working with Jessica and her husband, which has now led into a prosperous business relationship and deeply meaningful friendship.

Anyone who knows Jessica knows how much passion and drive she puts into her work every day. She's an advocate for mental health and overall well-being and uses her expertise in fitness, business, and physiology to educate others. Over the years, Jessica has taught me many valuable tools and provided insights about her personal experiences with anxiety and mental health. Two of the things I admire most about Jessica is her unwavering resilience and her dedication to helping others on their wellness journey.

Jessica has created this book with YOU and YOUR family in mind. Taking care of your mental health is important at every stage of life, from childhood and adolescence through to adulthood and parenthood. Mental health encompasses your overall psychological and emotional well-being, including your ability to cope with trauma. In this book, she pulls from her own family's experiences with mental health and trauma to offer readers effective tools to help manage anxiety.

When it comes to overall well-being, Jessica continuously enriches the lives of others, including my own, with her valuable insights and helpful strategies. When you read this book, she will enrich yours, too!

Reanna Alexander
Executive Assistant, Terri Hastings Real Estate Group/Keller Williams Realty Centres
Executive Assistant, Cedar Wellness Studio

INTRODUCTION

Hi! I'm Jess, and I'm so excited to share with you the tools I've learned from my family's experience with anxiety and what has helped our kids with managing their anxiety about school. Outside of being a mom of three and a wife to an amazing husband, I'm a certified recovery coach with YogaFit, a 500-CYT yoga instructor with YogaFit, and am certified in Warriors Trauma-Sensitive Yoga Teacher training as well as yoga therapy. I'm also a huge mental health advocate, and I'm incredibly excited to have been named one of Canada's Top Fitness Instructors of 2023 by Impact Magazine.

BACKGROUND

After beginning my search for help and support with anxiety, it quickly became evident that information related to children and managing their anxieties about school was not readily or easily available to parents or caregivers. My goal for this book is to share an easy-to-read guide with you containing helpful tools that I have learned over the many years of gathering information and working alongside professionals, so you and your family can begin using these anxiety-managing tools right away!

Our family's experience with anxiety began when my dad passed away suddenly. This traumatic, unexpected life change took me and my family many years to recover from, and it's still something we continue to heal from today. Grieving and recovery is a cycle, as I have come to learn, and we move through various phases of that cycle over time. When my dad passed, my oldest son was just starting junior kindergarten, and my daughter was only three months old. My family was so excited for my son's first official day of school. In preparation, my son and I went "back-to-school" shopping, we called grandma to talk about our "first-day outfit," and we tested out his new light-up shoes.

We were also nervous because we didn't know exactly how my dad's recent passing would affect my son and our family's emotional well-being and mental health in regards to him starting school. Surprisingly, his first day was a huge success! It wasn't until about a week into school that my husband and I started to notice a substantial change in our four-year-old son's personality and behaviour. Feelings of anxiety had started to set in. He no longer wanted to walk into school on his own, and he was terrified when I left after dropping him off at school.

So, our journey began in search of strategies to help him feel safe at school again. I was desperate to help him, so I dove in head first. I spent years working with counsellors, psycho-therapists, teachers, mental health coaches, and business coaches collecting and building a comprehensive toolbox of strategies for helping my children cope with their anxiety. I have also determined the best methods for teaching my kids *how* to access their *own* toolbox of strategies for managing anxiety. My husband and I now have two boys and one girl, two of which are attending public school regularly. Here are some of the tools that have worked for me and my family.

#1

SETTING THE FOUNDATION

SETTING THE FOUNDATION

To set the foundation for ourselves and our kids, there are a few strategies that we employ as a family on a regular basis. Some of these strategies have come from trial and error, while others are suggestions I came across while personally researching tools for accessing a state of "groundedness" or "feeling centered" that is not evident while in an anxious state. When we can set up a few simple resources for foundational grounding, we are better equipped to use these resources even when under pressure or duress that comes with an anxious experience. The more we can practice these strategies, the easier they will become to access, even without consciously thinking about putting them into practice. This is because we have trained our brain and built our neuro-pathways using these strategies, and they become automatic over time. They become subconscious tools that, when utilized, can have a big impact when it comes to returning to a calmer state of mind.

Here are three of the tools we use regularly with our own kids to help them find peace in grounding and stillness if they start to notice they are feeling uneasy.

FEELING GROUNDED

An easy tool my entire family, including our three-year-old son, uses regularly when we are feeling anxious or frustrated is rubbing the tips of our fingers together. I won't dive too deep into the psychology behind it,[1] but this motion helps us to feel centered and grounded. My kids like to rub the tips of their fingers with their thumb and slide their thumb back and forth across their fingers. This is a very simple tool they can use on their own wherever and whenever they feel worried or anxious, and it requires nothing but their fingers. This tool is both accessible and very effective. I often notice our kids making these motions with their fingers all on their own when they are feeling anxious.

BREATH

It's so important to teach our kids how to breathe correctly. It can be extremely scary for a young child when they feel their breath getting faster and shorter, and they don't understand why or what to do next.

When we turn our attention to *how* our kids are breathing, we may notice that they hold their breath in or breathe irregularly when feeling anxious. When we began to pay attention to our daughter's breathing, we noticed that she would take two small breaths in followed by an exhale whenever she was feeling worried. This type of irregular breath is a sign that their nervous system is not centered.[2] Breathing all our breath in and all our breath out, in and out through the nose, when we start to feel anxious will help centre our nervous system. I recommend repeating this type of breath five times when we start to feel like we are not centered.

There are different types of breaths for managing different types of emotions. We recommended our oldest son to use a different type of breath than the one described above. We encouraged him to take five deep breaths and start to lengthen his exhale each time in the morning when he sits up before getting out of bed. This type of breath helps to support the nervous system to rest and digest.[3] I am certain that our children will feel empowered once they have mastered their breathing! Mastering their breath shows them that they are in control and will help them to self-regulate their body and mind when they are feeling anxious. Every child is different, so these specific types of breath may not work best for everyone. Our son uses a longer, gentler breath to ground himself. However, this type of breath does not work for our daughter, so we encouraged her to use a stronger breath when exhaling (imagine the force it takes to fog up a window) because of the way we observe that she internally stores her emotions. Another type of breath that works well for our family is sighing. Sighing is the body's way of returning to centre.[4] Inhale all breath in and exhale to sigh it out. You will see the stress we hold in our shoulders start to release when we sigh it out. To prepare your kids for returning to school, I recommend practicing a variety of different breath types and styles that they can use when feeling anxious.

PERMISSION TO FEEL

This tool is so important. It is important that as parents we create a safe and open space for our kids to feel anything they want or need to. Over the years, I've come to learn that children may hold in their feelings out of fear of punishment or simply because they don't know what to do with them. When we set a foundation of mutual respect and trust with our kids, we create a safe environment for them to share their feelings. We need to let them know that all feelings are valid, so they will start to share when they are ready. It's important to validate them, to reiterate that they are important, and that we value who they are as a person in all ways. Something

I remind our kids of all the time is that we love them no matter what, even when they are mad, happy, sad, irritable, or excited!

I remember one night while putting my oldest to bed, I reminded him that his feelings matter, and he responded back with, "Thanks, Mom. I needed to hear that today." When we offer a safe space to express feelings, it helps our kids to keep their focus on school instead of spending their energy battling their own mind throughout their day.

———

These three simple strategies, when named and explained, can help our kids to feel supported and guided even in moments of uncertainty. We practice these strategies with our kids so frequently that they have become accustomed to pulling them out of their toolbox whenever they need to, even without our guidance. Start with a solid foundation, and the rest can build with much more ease and flow.

#2

TIPS TO USE IN A SCHOOL SETTING

TIPS TO USE IN A SCHOOL SETTING

Generating some clarity around regular school routines can be such a great tool to assist with your kids' familiarity and comfort levels before they enter the classroom and social environment of the school. The more familiar you and your children are with what's going to happen on a daily basis, the more comfortable they can become as their start date looms closer, especially if they have been feeling anxious leading up to what can be a momentous occasion for new (or returning) students. The following tips are geared towards helping kids to prepare and continue to manage the anxiety that could come from entering the school environment.

ROLE PLAYING

Every year during the last week of summer holidays, we practice getting back into our normal school routines. We get up early and go to bed early. We also do our morning school routine, drive to the school, and practice walking to the outdoor line-up spot. Practicing these routines ahead of time helps to encourage familiarity with the new environment and creates a feeling of safety in the body.[5] We even plan where we will play at recess each day and with which friends. We practice walking to different areas on the playground and role playing with our kids so that they will feel more comfortable when the time comes to pick a recess activity and a friend.

We also do a variety of verbal role-playing exercises with our children, so they can test out their social skills in a variety of different scenarios that may include their friends, teacher, or other students. Together we preview what subjects our kids want to talk about and why, and then offer simple words or phrases for them to use in their conversations. We also break down a prospective conversation into two or three parts for them, so it doesn't feel as overwhelming. This tool has tremendously helped my children feel more comfortable when engaging socially in a school setting. You will slowly start to notice your children's confidence grow from using this tool to prepare for social interactions on their own!

ORGANIZE RECESS

For many years, we've helped our kids organize which friend(s) they played with during their recess breaks. We continued this practice until our children felt confident enough to approach a friend on their own and ask them to play. Before we implemented this tool, I was shocked to hear from their teachers how often our kids played alone at recess only because they were too shy to ask someone to play with them or couldn't decide where to go on the playground. I can only imagine how many other kids struggle with the exact same thing. If this is something that you know your child struggles with, I recommend reaching out to your child's teacher and to other parents of the kids in your child's class to facilitate those connections. I know firsthand through my family's personal experiences that our children's teachers really do want to help their students feel confident and calm at school.

TOUR YOUR CHILD'S CLASSROOM BEFORE THE FIRST DAY BACK

This is a common tool that our family uses before every new school year starts. This can be as easy as calling the office and arranging an appointment to visit the school with your child. The teacher and school staff are usually more than willing to make an appointment available. This is probably one of the most important tools we've implemented for easing our children's anxiety about heading back to school. Not only does it show our kids exactly where their space will be for the upcoming school year, it also promotes a sense of familiarity in their mind and body on their first day of school. Remember that the mind and body crave familiarity because they want to feel safe.[6] By encouraging familiarity first in a low-key setting, we can lessen their feelings of uncertainness about the impending first day of school.[7]

Another strategy my children's psychotherapist recommended was for us to take pictures of the classroom and other school spaces during our visit, so the kids had something to review at home as many times as necessary. I think it's important to note here that whenever we need or request assistance from the school, we always ask kindly and respectfully. Don't underestimate how far a little kindness will go.

SEND A FAMILIAR ITEM TO SCHOOL WITH THEM

Over the many years of searching for strategies to lessen my children's anxiety, we discovered that allowing them to pick out an item of their choice to bring to school with them can help them feel more comfortable. Some examples of items our kids have chosen include a squeeze toy, a picture they value, and pop-it bracelets. Familiar items like these help to shift their energy when they start to feel anxious. It's important to mention that we do establish some boundaries with them and also let their teachers know why they have the item. I have also learned that the type of item will change alongside their age and interests. When my kids were younger, a squeeze toy was the most popular item they chose to bring with them to school.

ROUTINE

It's important to have an after-school routine and a before-school routine. This is something that your children will grow to expect and helps to create a smooth transition from before and after school to home. Our morning routine starts with getting up early enough to do all the things we need to do, which includes eating breakfast, showering, brushing our teeth, and getting ready for the day. For our family, we have learned to break up the tasks in the morning, and it has helped tremendously. For example, we have learned that it is better to have my husband help our daughter pick out clothes while I make lunches. When there are five of us to get ready in the morning, it can be overwhelming at times. This routine of who does which tasks is very helpful, and our kids know who to ask for what.

For our after-school routine, we allow one hour of down time where our children can do any activity they want after school. Our son often chooses soccer, and our daughter chooses to colour or play with her dolls. We then eat dinner, finish any outstanding homework, and get ready to go to whatever extracurricular activity we have scheduled for that evening, if any. Lastly, before bed we always take time to talk about our day. For us, this last part is a must because I have noticed my kids tend to release their feelings at bedtime. We talk about situations that bothered them or jokes they found funny. I let them lead the conversation. I am simply there to listen, offer guidance if asked, and assure them that their feelings are valued and valid. I know every family operates differently, but I encourage you to make this important time with your kids a priority.

The name of the game here is comfort. I've seen my own kids become so much more comfortable and confident in their entry to school each year, and I've observed their ongoing success in building and maintaining relationships with teachers and students alike when they employ these tips to feel as comfortable as possible with the over-all school experience. Being comfortable is being safe, and that's what we want.

#3

GENERAL TIPS FOR EVERYDAY USE

General Tips for Everyday Use

The following tips and suggestions work well for children in any scenario or situation, and we use these often with our own kids to help them find ways to feel more safe and secure when they notice anxious thoughts or feelings beginning to arise. It is remarkable when kids start to name how they are feeling, and it is one of the best gifts they can give them-selves...and one that you can help teach and facilitate as a parent or guardian as well.

Chewing Gum

Chewing gum when we feel anxious, stressed, or worried is a very popular tool to manage anxiety that even many adults can use as well as children.[8] I always make sure to carry gum everywhere we go. Chewing gum helps to release stress that is stored in the jaw, which is one of the main areas where we tend to hold our stress.[9] In fact, if my child is visibly becoming frustrated or sad, I offer them a piece of gum to kickstart the stress release process before they have even verbalized their feelings to me. Since implementing this tool, I have noticed that my kids will ask for gum when they are anxious without me even having to offer it, which shows that they now recognize the effectiveness of this tool. I know children are often not allowed to chew gum at school, so my children use this strategy before and after school and on the weekends.

CREATIVITY

I know everyone has those long days where they feel like all they are doing is holding it together until 5:00 p.m. or until the last bell rings! Children are no different. There are days I have picked up my kids from school and realize that they have been holding in tears since something happened that morning, which probably feels like an eternity to them. When we experience days like this (and we all do!), this is when we can get creative with the rest of our day. As parents, we can cook our child's favourite meal, take a family bike ride, or play their favourite board game—all of which will help to ease their nervous system back to rest and digest.[10]

Another tool I use is if I sense my child is feeling overwhelmed from school, I will often offer to pick them up early from school for a special "date." These dates can include going for a walk, grabbing a treat at a local coffee shop, or sitting on a park bench together and talking. Another option I've tried is taking them out of school for lunch. Although this strategy did work, the after lunch drop-off back at school did not always go smoothly, so we decided not to continue with this strategy for a couple years. Now that our son is older, he is much more confident when leaving and returning to school after a lunch date with his mom, so we've reimplemented this tool.[11]

TAPPING FINGERTIPS

Another strategy we have taught our kids to use when they are anxious is tapping.[12] "Tapping, or EFT, is a mind-body therapy that draws on the traditional Chinese medicine practice of acupuncture, and it is used today as a self-help approach in modern psychology. It involves tapping key acupressure points (acupoints) on the hands, face, and body with your fingertips while focusing on uncomfortable feelings or concerns and using positive affirmations to neutralize those feelings, according to EFT International. Research suggests that EFT tapping can relieve stress, diminish cravings, improve performance, and even help relieve symptoms of post-traumatic stress disorder (PTSD)."[13]

Tapping certain meridians, which are most easily defined as energetic highways in the human body, helps to calm the nervous system when we are stressed.[14] Although my children prefer not to tap at school, we do offer a safe space for them to tap at home anytime they like. They often choose to tap around bedtime. While tapping, we talk about what we feel happening inside our body and what it means. My daughter loves it, and it can be fun, too. Since we've started tapping, she can now recognize a strange feeling in her body and accept that although she can't identify it, she is able to understand there's something going on in there.

Teaching our kids to be more aware of their own body can help them to determine which strategies work best for their needs. To learn more about tapping, scan the QR code below or visit *youtube.com/@cedarwellnessstudio8293*

ESSENTIAL OILS

What *are* essential oils, anyway? "Essential oils are compounds extracted from plants, and they are often used in aromatherapy, a form of alternative medicine that employs plant extracts to support health and well-being."[15] It is important to look for high-quality options from reputable companies when it comes to incorporating essential oils, as

the effectiveness of using them for aromatherapy or any other corresponding support
techniques will be greatly diminished if
they are not of high quality and standard.

Essential oils are a big part of our household.
Although we're not able to send our kids to
school with oils, we do use them before and
after school and at bedtime. My kids now
know if they're feeling sad or have injured
their knee, their first go-to is asking for an
essential oil. What I love about this tool is
that my kids know the tool exists and can
verbally ask for it. Before school, we usually
put a dab of oil on their wrist or chest, and I
notice they look calmer and ready for their
day almost immediately. If you are inter-
ested in implementing essential oils into
your daily routine, please talk to an expert
as there are certain oils children should
refrain from using. I'm extremely lucky to
have expert friends who have taught me
the dos and don'ts of essential oils.[16] And,
if absolutely nothing else, we really and
truly enjoy the calming scents that come
from the essential oils we use and the added

comfort they can provide for us if and when we are looking for some calming support.

WELLNESS REGIME

Creating a wellness regime for your children can greatly decrease their levels of anxiety. Of course, my husband and I both enjoy massages, reflexology, osteopathy, physiotherapy, exercise, and sports, so why shouldn't we include our children in our wellness regime? Since coming to this realization, we've begun booking wellness appointments for our kids to enjoy as well. Every few months, all three of my children have a reflexology appointment with a professional who works with kids, where they get cranial sacral massages and regular massages. I now regularly jog alongside my oldest son, and he often joins me in our wellness studio to explore different exercises. I practice yoga with my daughter and youngest son, and they both love it! I also take my children to an osteopath who works with kids, and I'm amazed at what I have learned from them. Practicing wellness is not only healthy for parents but also for their children, too.

PUPPETS

Another neat strategy that can be found in my family's toolbox is working with puppets that have moving mouths. The goal is to use the puppets for role playing with the kids when they have a scenario they want to work through with us in a safe place. For example, I gave my daughter a puppet and asked her to act out how she was feeling when she couldn't find the words on her own. It was quite interesting to see her start to open up as soon as she started using the puppet. I want to note that it was quite difficult to find puppets with mouths, but it is important they have that feature. I believe this strategy is highly effective, especially because I've noticed that the schools also use this strategy to speak to the kids about important topics such as mental health.

TRIGGERS

I've learned that it's very important to get to know your child's triggers. What makes them feel anxious or stressed? For our son, it's loud noises and repetitive sounds. I can immediately see his stress levels change, and the anxiety starts to set in. Here are some strategies we've implemented to manage these triggers at school and at home.

When he was younger, at school his teacher offered earphones for him to use to avoid potential triggers. We also created a quiet area with pillows in his classroom that was always available if he needed a quiet space to work. Although he didn't take advantage of these tools at the time, I believe just knowing those resources were available for him to use if needed allowed him to feel more at ease. At home, we encourage our son to change his activity or location in the house if a certain noise begins to bother him. He now takes responsibility for his own triggers and can acknowledge his feelings surrounding them. When it comes to my daughter, being the perfectionist that she is, her triggers include making any kinds of mistakes. When this happens, she now knows to take a break, ask for a hug, or take a deep breath. Watching our kids struggle with their triggers is hard; however, I always feel reassured when I remember they are learning to move themselves forward by working through a problem on their own. A teacher said to me once: "These struggles are important, so they learn how to manage them on their own." And after hearing this, I understood what she meant and thought that made a ton of sense.

UNDERSTANDING THE AMYGDALA IN KIDS

What you may or may not know is that our amygdala performs a primary role in our emotional responses, which includes our fear and anxiety responses.[17] I have taught my children that the amygdala has an important function in the body. It helps to keep the body and mind healthy. When we get stuck in an anxious or fearful emotional response, one thing we can do is talk ourselves up to help bring our emotional state back to neutral. This is somewhat of a tricky tool to explain to kids, as you can imagine. This is what worked for me when I tried to explain it to my oldest son: Your AMY, short for amygdala, works to keep you and your body safe and healthy, and so we must always tell AMY how great it's doing. Additionally, we can talk with AMY as our friend to work together instead of against each other. It's pretty cool that after I taught my kids about the unconscious brain, one of them came home after school the very next day and let me know they cheered their AMY on during a difficult task. This helps children develop skills to have self-awareness and work with their fight or flight response rather than be overwhelmed by it, controlled by it, or afraid of it. My life coach Dianne Jamieson has coached me on using this tool and how to explain it to our kids. Her knowledge and understanding of "Taming AMY" is a brilliant tool to have and full credit must go to her as she helps create awareness in this area.[18] She's everything amazing!

MINDSET

Through my personal experiences as a business owner, I have learned that mindset is one of the most important tools we can teach our children. My husband and I take our mindset very seriously and are constantly learning new ways to improve our mindset. My husband starts his morning every day by meditating, journaling, going for a run, and showering. I start by meditating, reading a book, reflecting, going for a walk in nature, and then exercising. As a meditation and breath instructor, I get so excited when my kids and husband join me for meditations and breathing exercises. I love leading by example and exposing my children to healthy practices from a young age.

My children all have journals, and they are encouraged to write in them every morning before school. This tool allows them to get some of their feelings out, so they can start the school day on a calm, positive note. Lastly, we always work on our one-year and five-year goals as a family. My oldest two are old enough now to understand what this means and have written out their goals. And as a family, we go over them once a week. We teach our kids to visualize their goals, and the fun part is to watch them succeed in their goals! It's something to celebrate!

We must be our own best advocates when it comes to sensing how we feel and deciding what we need in order to move to a better state if anxiety is creeping in. Self-awareness is something we can all benefit from learning, knowing, and practicing, and kids can and will take their cues from their role models. Figuring out what tools and strategies work best for *you* as well as for *them* will make a world of difference in the entire family dynamic. As a family, we are regularly practicing our communication skills (with ourselves as well as with each other) in order to model good strategies and techniques for finding some reprieve when our circum-stances or environment may be causing us to feel uneasy. I promise that if you work on this yourself, it will not only benefit *you*, but it will have a massive positive impact on your kids and everyone else in your circle.

CONCLUSION

Overall, I believe it's important to continue exploring different tools to help manage or decrease feelings of anxiousness in our children and to remember that if some strategies are not working now, they may work later. In time, with the correct set of tools in place, your child's anxiety will become easier to manage, and they will start to trust in their ability to regulate and understand their own feelings and body. As parents, one of our main goals is to support our kids both when we are with them and when we are not. The best thing we can do is to teach our kids how to use these tools on their own. When they practice using these strategies independently and begin to realize they have the power to soothe their own body and mind, both you and your kids will feel empowered! It's exciting to watch our children use their tools on their own!

A special note to all the parents and caregivers reading this: you are doing amazing and need to give yourself credit for being willing to explore new opportunities to learn! Great job! I also want to extend a special thank you to my mom, Terri Hastings, for supporting my family through our journey of grief and anxiety as well as Dianne Jamieson, a keynote speaker, facilitator, and an incredible life coach who has taught me so much in mindset and the brain! Also, thank you to Robin Alexander, a young academic currently working in the legal sphere who has continuously cheered me along and helps bring my ideas to life, and her sister Reanna Alexander, who shares a special place in my heart as we would not be where we are today without the help and support Reanna has given to our kids. All of these women continue to support my desire to share my knowledge with all of you, and I couldn't be more appreciative of their help.

REFERENCES

1. Singh Khalsa, Dharma M.D., and Cameron Stauth. *Meditation As Medicine. Pocket Books*, 2001.

2. Singh Khalsa, Dharma M.D., and Cameron Stauth. *Meditation As Medicine. Pocket Books*, 2001.

3. Cooks-Campbell, Allaya. "Breathwork: The Secret to Emotional Regulation." *BetterUp*, 19 Aug. 2021, www.betterup.com/blog/breathwork?hs_amp=true. Accessed 23 May 2023. & Bullock, Grace. "What Focusing on the Breath Does to Your Brain." *Greater Good Magazine*, 31 Oct. 2019, greatergood.berkeley. edu/article/item/what_focusing_on_the_breath_ does_to_your_brain. Accessed 23 May 2023.

4. Ramirez, Jan-Marino. "The Integrative Role of the Sigh in Psychology, Physiology, Pathology, and Neurobiology." *National Library of Medicine*, 1 Jan. 2014, pubmed.ncbi.nlm.nih. gov/24746045/. Accessed 23 May 2023.

5. "The Importance of Schedules and Routines." *Head Start Early Childhood Learning & Knowledge Centre*, 10 Jun. 2022, eclkc.ohs.acf. hhs.gov/about-us/article/importance-sched-ules-routines. Accessed 23 May 2023.

6. Preisler, Jeanne. "Being Safe Vs. Feeling Safe." ***Fostering Perspectives***, 1 May 2013, fosteringperspectives.org/fpv17n2/psycho-logical-safety.html. Accessed 23 May 2023.

7. "5 Ways to Make a Child Feel Safe and Secure." *Choices Psychotherapy*, 18 Mar. 2018, choicespsychotherapy.net/5-ways-make-a-child-feel-safe-and-secure/. Accessed 23 May 2023.

8. Beyer, Anna Lee, and Debra Sullivan Ph.D, MSN, R.N. "Chew on These Facts: 9 Benefits of Chewing Gum." *Greatist,* 29 Oct. 2021, greatist.com/health/benefits-of-chewing-gum. Accessed 23 May 2023.

9. Rees, Mathiew, and Nicole Washington DO, MPH. "What to Know about Jaw Tension and Anxiety." *Medical News Today*, 6 Jul. 2022, www.medicalnewstoday.com/articles/jaw-tension-anxiety. Accessed 23 May 2023.

10. "Balancing Your Nervous System." *Evolution Physical Therapy and Yoga,* 15 Dec. 2017, evolutionvt.com/balancing-nervous-system/. Accessed 23 May 2023.

11. "47 Practices to Heal a Dysregulated Nervous System." *Heal Your Nervous System,* 4 Nov. 2022, healyournervoussystem.com/47-prac-tices-to-heal-a-dysregulated-nervous-system/amp/. Accessed 23 May 2023.

12. "Do You Know the Difference between EFT and Tapping?" *Tapping with Dani*, 1 Jan. 2023, www.tappingwithdani.com/eft-tapping. Accessed 23 May 2023.

13. Bedosky, Lauren, and Justin Laube MD. "What Is EFT Tapping? A Detailed Scientific Guide on Emotional Freedom Technique." *Everyday Health*, 9 Nov. 2022, www.everydayhealth.com/wellness/eft-tapping/guide/. Accessed 30 Mar. 2023.

14. Daniels, Elayne M.D. "5 Things to Know About Tapping For Anxiety and Depression." *Dr. Elayne Daniels,* 23 Mar. 2023, drelaynedaniels.com/5-things-to-know-about-tapping-for-anxiety-and-depression/. Accessed 23 May 2023.

15. West, Helen. "What Are Essential Oils, And Do They Work?" *Healthline*, 30 Sept. 2019, www.healthline.com/nutrition/what-are-essential-oils. Accessed 30 Mar. 2023.

17. Guy Evans, Olivia, and Saul Mcleod Ph.D. "Amygdala Function And Location." *Simply Psychology*, 12 May 2023, www.simplypsychology.org/amygdala.html#:~:text=The%20amygdala%20is%20primarily%20involved,emotions%20like%20fear%20or%20pleasure. Accessed 23 May 2023.

18. Diane Jamieson, https://www.linkedin.com/in/jamiesondianne/

CERTIFICATIONS + COURSES REFERENCED

YogaFit for Warriors, 2016
Levine, Peter A., and Gabor Mate. *In an Unspoken Voice: How the Body Releases Trauma and Restores Goodness. North Atlantic Books*, 2010.

YogaFit for Healing Physical and Emotional Trauma, 2017
Emerson, David, and Elizabeth Hopper. *Overcoming Trauma Through Yoga: Reclaiming Your Body. North Atlantic Books*, 2011.

YogaFit for Pranayama, the Science and Practice of Breath and Cultivating Prana, 2011
Rosen, Richard. *The Yoga of Breath: A Step-by-Step Guide to Pranayama. Shambhala*, 2002.

ABOUT THE AUTHOR

Jessica Hastings-Lesperance is a renowned entrepreneur, certified yoga and fitness instructor, and dedicated mother of three. With a strong passion for empowering others and a relentless drive for success, Jessica is the founder of Cedar Wellness Studio, where she inspires individuals to unlock their full potential and embrace an extraordinary life.

Beyond her role at the studio, Jessica is a co-owner, Realtor®, and Director of Operations at The Terri Hastings Real Estate Group, Keller Williams Realty Centres. Her innovative mindset and penchant for creative marketing have positioned her as a trailblazer in the industry, constantly pushing boundaries and embracing unconventional ideas.

With an unwavering commitment to personal growth and the betterment of others, Jessica brings a wealth of expertise and experience to her ventures. Her entrepreneurial spirit and ability to transform passions into reality make her a truly inspirational figure in the business world.

Through her diverse endeavours and unwavering dedication, Jessica Hastings-Lesperance continues to impact the lives of countless individuals, leaving an indelible mark on both the wellness and real estate industries. Sign up for free tips for managing stress, meditation activities, and VIP perks at cedarwellnessstudio.ca.

You can find Jess on social media and on her website,

🌐
cedarwellnessstudio.ca

📷
@cedar.wellness.studio

f
cedarwellnessstudio

▶
@cedarwellnessstudio8293

www.ingramcontent.com/pod-product-compliance
Lightning Source LLC
Chambersburg PA
CBHW070942120626
46546CB00004B/1523